JANUS

(aka January)

A SEASON FOR THOSE WHO KNOW BETTER

JANUS
(aka January)
A SEASON FOR THOSE WHO KNOW BETTER

Published by Ink-Twenty
Richmond, VA
Email: ink-twentystudio@inktwentypublishing.com

First edition: December 13, 2025

ISBN: 9798993554471

CHAPTER ONE — The Doorway Month

Before the calendars flip and the last ornament is finally tucked away, before anyone starts reciting resolutions like they're auditioning for a self-help commercial, we pause to salute the original two-faced multitasker: Janus, Roman god of doorways, thresholds, and impeccable timing.

Janus is the kind of deity you'd want at a party — one face politely receiving guests and the other already scouting the dessert table. One face looks back, not with guilt but with the amused, slightly reproachful air of someone who's seen your holiday jazz hands and knows exactly which ornament you broke but artfully never mentioned. The other face looks forward, squinting toward the horizon with a private notebook titled, Possibilities. He stands in the doorway like a maître d' of time, holding the door open with a flourish and asking, with gentle mischief, "Well? In or out?"

And there you are, perched on that threshold. Not clinging to the past, not vaulting headlong into the future — simply lingering in the delicious in-between. One shoe dusted with December glitter, the other on the fresh, unscuffed floor of the New Year. You take a breath. You decide whether to carry the baubles forward or leave them on the mat.

No month wears symbolism with such theatrical flair. December sparkles and insists on sentimentality. April sneezes and flirts with rebirth. July arrives with a marching band and a barbecue. January? January introduces the whole show. It doesn't demand a costume change; it hands you a program and a wink and says, "Pick your role."

Now for the good question — the one you either brush aside or answer dramatically in the shower: Did you fight those traditions, or did you make a little magic of your own?

If your holidays read like a well-executed Broadway revival — same cues, same relatives in the same chairs, same song heard at least five times — kudos. Tradition has its comfort; it's the steady rhythm your life tuned itself to. But if you found yourself quietly rebelling at 2 a.m. — swapping eggnog for tea, hiding a fragile ornament in plain sight, or inventing a new dessert so someone would finally stop making that cake no one likes — congratulations. You innovated. You improvised. You practiced modern ritual.

Because here's the truth: you've had a life. A full one. A layered one. You've collected habits like good china and stories like postcards. January isn't about "getting your life together" — that phrase belonged to a poster you probably owned in 1989. No, this month is a very different kind of gift: permission. Permission to keep what glows and shelve what sags under obligation. Permission to make the holidays fit your life rather than contort your life around them.

If you've run the holiday show for decades — cooked, chauffeured, corralled — you own certain secret competencies. You know how to make a living room sparkle with two lamps and a good throw. You can host without the theatrics and leave everyone feeling satisfied.

You can wrap a gift so neatly the recipient will be tempted to save the paper. You've earned the right to rewrite everything.

And rewrite we shall. But with style. With humor. With a little bit of mischief.

You'll notice, as you walk through January, two archetypal approaches. There's the audition approach — "New Year, New Me!" — performed with crisp yoga gear and high expectations. There's also the seasoned performance approach — "New Year, Same Me; Slight Adjustments" — a calmer, cheekier stance favored by those who have seen many Januaries and know they all end somewhere between competence and laughter.

Pick your posture. I recommend the latter, with optional confetti.

Let us be clear: January does not apologize. It arrives wearing a neutral palette and a serious face. It's chilly, blunt, and occasionally unromantic. And yet — beneath that frost — it keeps company with a determined, domestic kind of hope. Not the fireworks-and-confetti variety. Not the immediate-metamorphosis, three-steps-to-a-bigger-you commercial. This hope is quieter: an extra minute of daylight, a mug that feels right in your hand, a cleared path on a morning when the rest of the world sleeps in.

Take the weather, for instance. There is the cruel poetry of lake-effect snow — a body of water deciding you deserve novelty in the form of a surprise blizzard. One moment your driveway is a respectable driveway; the next it's a scene from a winter caper, and you are the unwilling lead. Weather, like family, will test your patience with relish. You can grumble, or you can invest in a decent shovel and a thermos of cocoa and call it character building.

And then there is the cultural suggestion du jour: Dry January. Two words that read like a dare typed in all caps. Somewhere, some wellness influencer with an attractive water bottle and a very clear lighting setup decided that the bleakest, coldest month was the ideal time to test willpower. Brave? Sure. Admirable? Maybe. Well-timed? Debatable.

If you're inclined to try a sober month, do so with theatricality: ceremoniously replace the wine rack with a curated shelf of fancy tonic waters and declare the library table a mocktail bar named "Second Chances." If you're not inclined, that's perfectly fine too. January doesn't come with rules; it comes with options dressed in sensible shoes.

Let's talk small rituals because those are the ones that actually stick. You don't need a manifesto to begin again. Begin with a mug, and then maybe another. Begin with a ten-minute walk. Begin with a single cleared counter. A small habit is a powerful friend. These micro-changes build the quiet scaffolding of a new season: the extra five minutes of sun that keep stacking until spring looks less like rumor and more like fact.

There is also a kind of boomer-specific magic: the learned art of doing less with better intention. After decades of orchestrating holidays that would have challenged a stage manager, many prefer editing to inventing. Keep the roast your mother made that always lands applause. Keep the song that gets everyone up dancing. Remove the obligation that comes with a guest list. Turn the holiday into a memory you want to make again — not a checklist you must complete because some outdated rulebook said so.

Small rebellions, when practiced with taste, are the most satisfying. Think of the neighbor who traded the formal Christmas dinner for diner pancakes on Boxing

Day. At first it felt like heresy. By year four, they didn't talk about turkey; they talked about cinnamon and the right way to fold a napkin. Tradition had been gently remixed into joy — and the book of family rituals welcomed a new page.

January also rewards those who rest without apology. There is an art to this: not laziness but curated ease. Learn it and you will be surprised how much ground you can gain while apparently doing nothing. Rest is not an absence of productivity; it is investment in clarity. Old hands at life know this: you cannot steward anyone else's joy if you have none for your own.

By the time you step fully into the month, you will have accumulated small victories that look suspiciously domestic: a label on a bin that clarifies Christmas ornaments from Halloween keepsakes; a cleared path to the herb pot on the windowsill; a phone call scheduled with an old friend because you once promised you would. These are not grand gestures. They are the quiet currency of a life well tended.

So here's the invitation, classic boomer style: walk through the door at your own pace. Bring a sweater. Bring a mug you love. Bring a smirk and a sensible plan. Do what you need to do to make January work for you — keep the parts that shimmer, send the rest gently to the attic, and maybe invent a little ritual of your own. The month is patient; it likes a confident guest.

Janus has bowed. The threshold held. The stage is lit. The scene is yours.

Walk through when you're ready.

CHAPTER TWO — The Art of the Put-Away Ceremony

January Boomer Style

Every generation cleans up after the holidays, but Boomers? Oh, Boomers have elevated it into an art form, a seasonal rite, a ritual that deserves its own soundtrack (preferably something from the Carpenters or a Motown playlist that has seen you through at least 300 cookie-baking cycles).

This is not "taking down decorations."
This is The Put-Away Ceremony — part tradition, part archaeology, part emotional inventory, part domestic theatre.

And it begins with the great unspoken truth:
What goes up with giddy enthusiasm in November comes down with a deep sigh in January.

But it does come down — lovingly, intentionally, with a practiced rhythm forged from decades of holiday survival.

The Lighting of the Lamp (a.k.a. Step One)
Every Put-Away Ceremony begins with the ritual flipping of a lamp. Not the overhead light — heavens no — but the good lamp, the one that casts a warm glow and makes you feel competent.

You place it where you can see every glittering remnant of December and say, with a calm, sovereign air, "All right. Let's do this."

If you want to be fancy about it, you may warm up the house with a pot of coffee or tea first. January, after all, is not a month for cold beverages unless you're drinking them under protest.

The Search for the Correct Bin

This step reveals your personal organizational philosophy.

You either:

Have a meticulously labeled set of matching bins, or

Have a chaotic stack of plastic containers in assorted colors that once held everything from artificial trees to children's science projects, and you view this mess as an adventure.

Both are honorable.

Both are traditional.

Both are distinctly Boomer.

You open each bin like a treasure chest:

Is this the nativity set? No, those are Easter napkins.

Is this the ornaments? No, that's Halloween 1997.

Ah — here's the tree skirt. Or at least... one of them.

The Ornament Archeology

There are two types of ornament-packing styles:

The Delicate Approach

Each ornament is wrapped tenderly in tissue paper or placed in its own little compartment like a Fabergé egg. As you pack them away, you remember who gave what and which child made that glitter monstrosity in 1974 that still sheds sparkles when you so much as look at it.

The Practical Approach

Everything gets wrapped in whatever soft material you have: paper towels, last week's newspaper, a scarf you no longer love, and maybe a sock with no mate. Efficiency triumphs. Nothing breaks. You're a domestic MacGyver.

Both methods are correct.

Both are a legacy.

The Annual Burnout Scavenger Hunt

This is when you evaluate which lights still work after 30 days of being plugged into every outlet with an extension cord that would make OSHA faint.

There is always:

one strand that flickers

one that is half-dead

one that works perfectly but tangles itself out of spite

You will promise yourself that next year you'll replace them.

You won't.

And that's fine. It's tradition.

The Tinsel Reckoning

If you used tinsel, you have accepted your fate.

You will find stray pieces until June. Possibly August.

Tinsel is like a festive houseguest who refuses to leave — charming in December, strangely loyal in March.

The Tree Farewell

Whether your tree is real, artificial, aluminum, flocked, slim, wide, pre-lit, or older than your mortgage, the moment it comes down is always a little bittersweet.

Real tree people must wrestle the thing out the door like an overgrown toddler resisting bedtime. Pine needles will follow you into the spring thaw.

Artificial tree people must coax the branches back into the box — a test of patience, geometry, and upper body strength.

If you stand on the box to close it, you're in excellent company.

The Sweep, the Sip, the Sigh

Once everything is stored and stacked (or balanced precariously) in its designated corner, you perform the final ritual:

A broom or vacuum

A mug of something warm

A long, satisfied exhale

And there it is — space.
A blank room.
A clean mantle.
A sense of calm so profound that you briefly consider writing a book about minimalism.

The January Quiet

When the decorations are gone, there is a stillness that only Boomers truly appreciate.
Not emptiness — clarity.

The house exhales.
You exhale with it.

This is where you settle into your own rhythm — the quiet hum of winter life, the soft return of routine, and the freedom to decide how you want this year to unfold.

Some people think January is dull. Those people have clearly never mastered The Put-Away Ceremony.

Because for Boomers, the magic isn't just in the holidays —
it's in the clearing, the resetting, the reclaiming of space and self.

And that, my friend, is how January really begins.

CHAPTER THREE

The Glory of Micro-Rituals

If January were a person, it would be the sort of guest who doesn't demand a whole itinerary — just a tiny, thoughtful courtesy that says, I see you. I brought a thermos. The month's superpower is its patience; it rewards small, steady acts more than any flaming, Instagram-ready reinvention. That, dear reader, is where micro-rituals shine.

Micro-rituals are tiny ceremonies with outsized returns. They don't require a committee, a casserole or a subscription box. They are three-minute practices with the soul of a spa retreat and the logistics of a habit you can actually keep. Think of them as tiny anchors in a season that sometimes feels like a slow-motion wardrobe change: you're still you, but the lining is new.

Why do these matter? Because huge change is exhausting; tiny change is sustainable. A micro-ritual is a polite nudge — not an accusation. It says: "You don't have to rewrite everything. You just need one good move." And often, that one move generously multiplies.

Herewith, a bouquet of micro-rituals — time-tested, slightly mischievous, and totally Boomer-approved. Pick one, three, or invent your own. The goal is not perfection; it's pleasure.

Cup of Dawn

Start with this: pour yourself a mug of something warm before the day starts making demands. Call it Cup of Dawn. It might be coffee, it might be tea, it might be something herbal that smells like hope and lavender. Sit by a window, watch the light do its small, steady work, and give yourself five quiet minutes. No emails, no to-do lists, no polite scrolling. Just that mug. The ritual stakes are low; the payoff is calm. Do this three times and the world will already feel like it's on your side.

The Ten-Minute Triage

Set a timer for ten minutes and do one small, stubbornly boring task. Fold a load of laundry. Empty the junk drawer. Put paprika back in its rightful home. It sounds trivial because it is — and that's the point. Ten minutes of focused completion creates a dopamine hit that sends your internal secretary a note: We are competent. Repeat daily and by month's end you will stare at your kitchen island and think, with suspicious pride, "I got this."

The First Drawer

Choose one drawer (not the junk drawer; we love the junk drawer) and turn it into The First Drawer. This is the place for small things that make life smoother: a spare pen that actually writes, a pair of scissors that cuts without drama, your trusty lip balm. Keep it tidy. When life gets slippery, opening The First Drawer should feel like finding fangirl-level treasures — simple, reliable tools that say, "Hello, practical joy."

The Sunday Five

This isn't religion; it's preparation. Every Sunday evening, pick five things to make the coming week gentler. It could be: preheat the oven before you leave, set out next day's outfit, schedule two phone calls (one business, one friend), and water the plant that insists on dramatic droopiness. Keep the list short. Keep it achievable. Watch how much lighter Mondays become when you cheat them a little.

The "No-Decision" Breakfast

Some mornings, the cognitive load of choosing cereal is too much. Declare once — in ink, if you like — a No-Decision Breakfast you will rotate through for the month. It could be the same good oatmeal with fruit every weekday and a small indulgence on Saturday. The charm here is not monotony; it's the economy of decision. Save your braincells for the things that matter (like whether to scroll the news).

The Memory Minute

Pick a time each day for a single, deliberate memory. Close your eyes for sixty seconds and reproduce a small, rich scene from your life — your father's laugh while carving the turkey, the sound of a child's squeal at seeing a tree, a small kindness someone once did. This is not nostalgia for the sake of it. It's a practice that trains gratitude and reminds you the archive of your life is pretty well stocked.

The Little Hello

Text someone a photograph of something that made you smile that day: the curious cat behind the curtains, a strange cloud, your neighbor's hat. No agenda. No expectations. Micro-rituals that involve other people are the secret sauce to winter cheer — they are tiny bridges that keep friendship warm without the pressure of planning a weekend.

The Pause Before the Phone

Make a rule: when you sit down, pause for a breath before you reach for the phone. It's astonishing how many moods are redirected by that one small delay. You will miss nothing important, and you might save yourself a swath of reactive irritation.

The Seasonal Edit

Once a week, for five minutes, pick something to release. One sweater that no longer feels like you. One plate you never use. One obligation that only drains you. The Seasonal Edit is minimalist in spirit (but not in feeling). It gives January its clean, crisp edges without demanding you become ascetic.

Small Rebellions, Practiced With Taste

Micro-rituals are also the domain of gentle mischief. Want to skip the big dinner and host a pancake party at noon? Do it. Want to send invites that say "BYOS: Bring Your Own Stories"? Go for it. Rules are often suggestions written in invisible ink. A well-executed small rebellion becomes a tradition after year three.

A Note on Habit and Grace

Habits often sound like strict regimens; micro-rituals are subtler. They are habits you like. If you miss them, no moralizing; simply start again the next day. The goal is warm constancy, not shrinking standards for your own humanity.

Micro-rituals help January do what it does best: make newness manageable. They are the spoonful of something sweet that lets you swallow the concept of "beginning again" without coughing. They provide scaffolding for the slow work of improvement while honoring the fact that life — by design — is imperfect and delightfully complicated.

So choose one. Name it. Claim it. And let it be the tiny thing that changes how the month feels.

CHAPTER FOUR

Weather as a Personality Test

January has always been a month with opinions — and none stronger than the weather's. If December is sentimental and sparkly, January is the blunt friend who tells you the truth whether you asked for it or not. The sky draws up a résumé of your inner character and starts conducting evaluations without warning: resilience, humor, layering strategy, ability to drive through precipitation that looks like wet powdered sugar. All scored, silently, by the elements.

The older you get, the more convinced you are that weather reveals a person's temperament more than astrology ever has. Sun signs may explain your confidence, but wind chill? Wind chill unveils your soul.

The Cold-Weather Philosopher

These are the ones who stand in the doorway in the morning, coffee in hand, narrating the weather like it's a PBS special. "Hmm. Thirty-two but feels like twenty-three. You can see the humidity in the air. Look at that cloudline — we're in for something." They say it with gravitas. They say it as if they were consulted.

Boomers often become Cold-Weather Philosophers because we've lived long enough to have experienced weather before apps tried to interpret it for us. Our weather report was once the newspaper, the evening anchor, and the pain in an uncle's knee. And honestly, it worked just fine.

The Stoic Layerer

This personality does not complain. Not about sleet, not about slush, not about the grim three-day stretch where the sun clocks out early and no one knows where it went. The Stoic Layerer simply adds another sweater and says, "It's fine," even when it clearly isn't.

This is the spirit that built generations. You survived winters before heated seats and instant defrost. You endured wind that could chap your face into a topographical map. You completed errands in coats so bulky you had to turn your whole body to look behind you. You learned fortitude from Sears catalog parkas.

January doesn't scare you; it just keeps things interesting.

The Weather Denier

A classic. This is the soul who steps outside in 18 degrees with a light jacket and says, "It's not that bad." It is that bad, but denial is a coping mechanism as old as the zodiac.

Many Boomers fall briefly into this category in mid-January — the danger zone where holiday adrenaline has worn off, but spring is still a rumor. You dress aspirationally, as if the universe might take the hint. It won't. Wear the scarf.

The Early-Warning Siren

Every friend group has one: the person who monitors radar like they're employed by the National Weather Service. They send screenshots, charts, bulletins, and dire warnings about "the system moving in" even when the system is a passing cloud.

These individuals peak during lake-effect season — that magical meteorological trick where snow appears out of nowhere simply because a large body of water feels mischievous. You don't need to mention geography; anyone who's lived through it knows. Snow that multiplies like rabbits. Storms that ignore forecasts. Skies that say, "You thought we were done? Oh, sweetie."

The Early-Warning Siren shines brightest here, bless them. Their vigilance is unmatched. Their group texts are long. Their timing is impeccable.

The Indoor Adventurer

This is the personality who responds to weather not by going out but by going in — deeper into comfort, deeper into cozy, deeper into nesting. The colder it gets outside, the more a Boomer indulges in the ancient art of putting on socks with grip dots and declaring, "I'm good right here."

- reorganizing the pantry like it's an archaeological dig
- rearranging furniture for the fourth time since Thanksgiving
- discovering a hobby that requires twelve bins
- beginning — and abandoning — a puzzle
- reading a book you forgot you bought because the cover looked "atmospheric"

Winter has always been your excuse to savor stillness long before "self-care" was a brand.

The Conversation Starter

Some people talk about weather because they have nothing else to say. Boomers talk about it because we have everything to say. Weather is the great equalizer —

universal, unpredictable, a relatable mess much like daily life. It's a shortcut to connection, a soft opening to conversation, a way of saying, "I see you, and I'm checking if your roof is still intact."

January brings out our best stories — blizzards we walked through, storms that canceled weddings, the year the snowplow buried the mailbox. These tales aren't complaints; they're badges of honor. Generational lore.

The Fair-Weather Rebel

These are the brave few who defy the forecast in style. They plan a winter picnic. They sit on the porch with a blanket and a mug just to prove they can. They find a sunny patch on a bitter day and stand in it like a solar panel charging its last bar. January respects this kind of stubborn cheer. It may not reward it, but it acknowledges it.

In the End, Weather Reveals Us

January weather brings out our personalities the way holidays bring out family dynamics — fully, loudly, and without apology. Whether you respond with grit, humor, practical layering, or cheerful defiance, winter is simply offering you a chance to see who you are today.

After all, you've lived through decades of seasons, storms, and unexpected forecasts. January has nothing on you — it's just another doorway to walk through, bundled and brilliant.

CHAPTER FIVE

Domestic Triumphs & Everyday Bravery

January is the month when the domestic arena becomes a battlefield and a sanctuary all at once. The holidays are over, the decorations are packed away, and suddenly the house is just yours again—to manage, to enjoy, to conquer… or occasionally to surrender to a well-earned nap.

The domestic victories of this month are rarely reported, rarely photographed, and often completely invisible. But Boomers know them intimately: these small feats, these clever hacks, these moments of quiet resilience, are the real triumphs of January.

The Laundry Marathon

Laundry in January is not just a chore—it is a test of endurance, logic, and memory. Towels, socks, winter layers, and scarves have accumulated like miniature snowdrifts. Sorting colors, fabrics, and mysterious lone gloves requires both patience and strategy.

Victory comes in stages:

- the first load completed without bleeding colors
- all socks paired and accounted for
- the warm, folded pile stacked neatly in the basket
- the realization that the machine has run more loads than a New Year's Eve countdown

This is everyday bravery, and it deserves applause. Bonus points if you folded a sweater correctly on the first try.

The Grocery Gauntlet

Walking into a store in January can feel like navigating a storm. Shelves are reset, seasonal displays hang over aisles like clouds of glittery confetti, and that one brand of coffee you rely on seems to have disappeared.

A domestic triumph here is small but satisfying:

- you remember reusable bags
- you dodge the display that wants to sell you kale in December
- you remember the butter

Success is measured not in Instagram likes but in the unspoken nod to yourself as you haul bags into the house, victorious.

The Forgotten Corner Rescue

Every home has one: a cabinet, closet, or shelf that silently collects the remnants of seasons past. January is the perfect month for small-scale heroism: rescuing forgotten tools, dusting shelves, rediscovering last summer's baking pans, or that spatula you swore had vanished forever.

The act is mundane, but the satisfaction is profound. It's a triumph because you are reclaiming control of your own space — a gentle but firm assertion that order and calm can exist again.

The Maintenance Mindset

Winter exposes household weaknesses: drafty windows,

dripping faucets, squeaky hinges. January becomes a month of vigilance.

- Tighten the loose knobs
- Oil the hinges
- Replace a burned-out bulb before it annoys you for a week

Every small fix is a win. Every minor adjustment is proof that you still understand your home, and that your home understands you.

The Cooking Confidence Boost
No holidays, no pressure, just meals that matter. Perhaps you rediscover the joy of a simple roast chicken, a pot of soup that smells like courage, or a dessert that doesn't need a reason beyond making you smile.

The bravery here is in trying again—whether that means flipping a pancake without a spatula mishap, or experimenting with an old recipe you once feared. In January, your kitchen becomes a lab for domestic skill and confidence, and every successful meal is a medal.

The Small-Scale Celebration
January may lack the sparkle of December, but it is not without its moments. Lighting a candle, arranging a fresh bouquet, or putting a small note on the fridge for yourself counts.

These micro-triumphs remind us that domestic life is not a series of chores—it is a canvas, and we are the artists. In a month that is often gray, these small, intentional acts of care bring color and light.

In Summary
Domestic triumphs are the unnoticed victories of January:

folding the laundry, conquering the pantry, rescuing forgotten corners, fixing what needed fixing, cooking with purpose, and celebrating the little things.

These are acts of bravery, because they require patience, perseverance, and a steady eye toward the quiet beauty of ordinary life.

In this month, the mundane becomes heroic, and the small victories — the ones we often forget to honor — become the threads that hold the rest of the year together.

CHAPTER SIX

Anecdotes & Small Triumphs

If Chapter Five celebrated the mechanics of domestic mastery, Chapter Six celebrates the stories that live in the margins of January. The anecdotes, the small victories, the moments that make a cold, gray month shimmer without anyone else noticing.

This is where life reveals its humor, its grace, and its surprising generosity — the kind that sneaks up when no one is watching, often accompanied by a mug of something warm, a favorite sweater, and the faint echo of laughter from another time.

The Accidental Masterpiece
You've all experienced it: you pull out the mixing bowl for some simple weekday task—cookies, soup, or pancakes —and something miraculous happens. The recipe doesn't just turn out; it surpasses expectations.

- The cookies are crisp on the outside, tender on the inside.
- The soup develops a richness you swear wasn't there last week.
- The pancakes flip perfectly, landing like tiny golden discs of glory.
- These small triumphs are accidental, but they remind you that domestic life contains its

own kind of magic. Sometimes the universe rewards attention to small details with delight you didn't even know you were capable of creating.

The Lost-and-Found Victory

There is no joy greater than finding something you swore had disappeared forever. A missing earring, the perfect spatula, a library book hiding behind the radiator.

Boomers know this deeply. After decades of accumulated stuff—gifts, heirlooms, kitchen gadgets, and memories—every rediscovery carries weight. It's not just the object; it's the confirmation that attention and persistence matter. That victory is possible even in the quietest corners of life.

The Calendar Coup

January brings an opportunity to reclaim time. One small triumph is scheduling things deliberately instead of reacting to the tyranny of the inbox or the whims of the world.

- A lunch with a friend you haven't seen in months.
- A morning walk that doesn't collide with errands.
- A quiet half-hour just to read, journal, or stare at the sky.

• Every intentional entry on the calendar becomes a triumph of foresight and self-respect. A quietly defiant assertion that you decide how time unfolds.

The Houseguest of One

Sometimes, the greatest victory is simply enjoying your own company. In the lull of post-holiday January, we often find ourselves with empty rooms and the freedom to roam without agenda.

• You curl up in a chair by the window, noticing the snow or the faint smell of winter pine.

• You brew another cup of coffee because you deserve it.

• You read a passage aloud to no one in particular because it pleases you.

• These are the victories of solitude — quiet, elegant, and entirely yours.

The Tech Taming

A small, modern triumph that any Boomer can appreciate is conquering technology that seemed determined to defeat you.

• Updating a phone or tablet without calling a teenager.

• Figuring out the streaming menu and actually finding the show you want.

• Sending a photo attachment correctly, on the first try.

• Each small success is a tiny battle won in the daily war against buttons, passwords, and pop-ups. And let's face it: it feels spectacular.

The Friendship Surprise

Triumphs aren't always solitary. The small gestures that

maintain friendship — calling, texting, sharing a joke or a link, showing up with coffee — are victories that ripple outward.

Even a tiny act — dropping off a loaf of bread for a neighbor, returning a book, or sending a "thinking of you" note — counts as a triumph of grace and connection.

Boomers have the advantage here: decades of friendship have taught us that consistency and warmth outweigh flashiness every time.

The Minor Miracle of Clean Spaces
A desk organized. A counter cleared. A closet sorted. A corner polished.

These small, physical victories carry an invisible weight of calm and order. There's something deeply satisfying about seeing a flat surface without clutter, a shelf without chaos, a home that hums instead of groans.

It is not perfection. It is not grand. But it is triumph.

The Smile That Arrives Unexpectedly
Finally, the smallest triumph may not even be something you do — it may be something that happens to you:

- A child laughs at a joke you've told a thousand times.
- A pet curls at your feet and refuses to move.
- A neighbor waves in a way that reminds you that the world still contains friendliness.
- These fleeting moments, often overlooked, are the proof that joy and victory can appear in the quietest spaces.

In Summary
Anecdotes and small triumphs are the gems hidden in the folds of January. They remind us that life's magic often

comes quietly, without fanfare, without an audience, and without expectation.

In the gray month of January, these tiny victories — the rediscoveries, the calm moments, the unexpected smiles — are the threads that create warmth, humor, and perspective.

They are the triumphs we carry into the next month, into the next season, into the rest of our lives.

CHAPTER SEVEN

Dry January (Or Not)

January arrives like that friend who shows up unannounced, clipboard in hand, ready to judge your life choices. Somewhere along the way, someone decided that this gray, cold, post-holiday month needed an extra challenge: Dry January. Skip the wine. Skip the cocktail. Be virtuous. Be pure. Be… bored?

For most Boomers, the concept is already laughable. After a season of eggnog, sparkling wine, and whatever dessert paired with spirits, sobriety is already at a discount. And now, like an unexpected blitz, January throws football into the mix: NFL playoffs. Suddenly, Dry January becomes a mythical creature — as rare and impossible to sustain as a snow-free midwinter in the Midwest.

Tailgating Reality Check

For fans whose teams are marching through the playoffs, the siren song of beer, chips, nuts, ribs, brats, and buffalo wings is unavoidable. The pre-game gathering in the parking lot (tailgate, yes, that sacred ritual) is a festival of indulgence, aroma, and camaraderie. Rules are optional. Moderation is a joke.

Dry January, in this context, is like chasing a unicorn on a frozen pond. You may want it, you may have written it down on Instagram in early December, but one whiff of bratwurst smoke and a passing tray of wings, and suddenly it's gone. Poof. Mythical. Legendary.

The Sober Rebel

Some Boomers meet this challenge with strategy: sip water between beers, nibble cautiously, or quietly proclaim, "I'm pacing myself," while secretly savoring just enough. This is the art of the Sober Rebel: clever, self-aware, slightly mischievous, and fully prepared to wink at the universe.

Others embrace the chaos. There is no shame in tasting the chili, polishing off a sausage, or cheering with a half-full glass. Hygge may demand comfort in a blanket at home, but football season demands solidarity — and sometimes that includes indulgence.

Instagram Virtue, Meet Reality

Meanwhile, social media is flooded with kale smoothies, sparkling water, and hashtags that scream moral superiority. Boomers have a quiet response: a small plate of cheese, a hidden sip of wine, and the satisfaction of knowing we have perspective. Deprivation is optional. Optional is negotiable. And sometimes, a beer in hand is simply life-affirming.

Victory Redefined

Success in January is no longer measured in unbroken streaks of sobriety, but in joy, warmth, and mischief managed with style. Watching your team advance, engaging in tailgate antics, and laughing at the absurdity of a "dry" month in the middle of playoff season? That is the real triumph.

Dry January is now a mythical creature. It exists in theory, in Instagram posts, in health blogs. But in practice? It steps aside politely as bratwurst, buffalo wings, and a cold beer march through the parking lot. And we, seasoned veterans of holidays, winters, and playoff

Sundays, smile knowingly, raise a glass, and choose our battles wisely.

January is long. The nights are cold. The beer is cold. And somewhere between the post-holiday lull and the playoff cheers, you realize: you make the rules. Dry January can try, but it doesn't stand a chance when joy, tradition, and a little rebellion are involved.

Raise a glass. Cheer loudly. Laugh often. Because in January, fun trumps virtue every time.

CHAPTER EIGHT

The Boomer Social Season: Winter Edition

Winter after the holidays has its own rhythm: the sparkle of December is gone, but the social invitations keep rolling in. Birthday parties, luncheons, playoff watch gatherings, and the occasional "let's catch up before the year disappears" appear like snowflakes—each one demanding charm, patience, and occasionally, strategic planning.

For Boomers, navigating these months is part skill, part humor, and part stubborn endurance. It's a season that tests patience while offering opportunities for small, satisfying victories.

The Invitation Avalanche

Keeping track of events can feel like a sport: who's hosting, what's expected, and whether you can RSVP without overcommitting. Sometimes it helps to see these invitations as tiny snowballs rolling toward you, gaining speed. Saying yes to everything is a trap; knowing when to say no is an art form honed over decades.

Small triumphs here include arriving on time, remembering names and stories, and leaving with laughter intact. These understated wins are quietly glorious— though rarely documented in photos.

Winter Wardrobe Warfare

Winter gatherings demand both warmth and style, a balancing act for anyone negotiating freezing sidewalks and social expectations. Layers are essential, boots must be practical but photogenic, and outerwear becomes armor for the elements. Elegance, humor, and a well-chosen scarf can transform even the grayest January day into an opportunity for understated brilliance.

Navigating the Food Terrain

Winter social gatherings often feature a landscape of snacks, coffee, desserts, and wine—an unspoken test of endurance and taste. Strategic pacing is essential: indulge in what delights you most, ignore what doesn't, and sometimes, make a small rebellion of bringing your own dish.

- A few notes for surviving the culinary gauntlet:
- Know your strengths: choose the food that makes you happiest, not the trendiest item on the table.
- Hydrate. Sometimes water is the secret weapon in January.

Savor small pleasures and quietly claim your victories—like finishing the perfect bite without sharing it.

Conversation Tightrope

Topics at winter gatherings can wander from politics to grandchildren, neighborhood news, or that one story everyone has heard at least three times. The art of social survival is knowing when to speak, when to listen, and when to redirect conversation with humor or a well-timed anecdote. Observing quietly can be just as rewarding as joining the fray—and wit often wins where patience alone would fail.

Mini-Victories

- Winter social season is packed with small, satisfying triumphs:

- Arriving without forgetting essentials
- Navigating parking lots like a pro
- Leaving while the energy is still high
- These quiet moments of competence, grace, and subtle humor are the understated glories of Boomer social life. They deserve recognition, if only to remind ourselves that elegance, humor, and a little mischief can make even January memorable.

In Summary

The winter social season is a blend of charm, strategy, and subtle rebellion. Boomers navigate it with wit, small victories, and attention to what really matters: connection, laughter, and leaving events on our own terms. Success isn't surviving every gathering—it's enjoying them with style, humor, and just enough cheek to make the season truly yours.

CHAPTER NINE

Resting Without Guilt

January is the perfect month to master the art of resting without guilt. After the frenzy of holidays, the social season, and perhaps a playoff game or two, the idea of downtime should feel like a crown placed gently upon your head. Yet somewhere along the way, society decided that doing nothing is suspicious, lazy, or "unproductive."

Boomers know better. We've seen enough of the world's chaos to recognize that rest is not a crime—it's survival, strategy, and sometimes, outright rebellion.

Claiming Space

Rest is not a passive act; it is an intentional one. Carve out corners of your home for quiet: a favorite chair, a window nook, a cozy blanket on the sofa. The very act of creating a sanctuary is a victory.

Here, the rules are simple:

• Silence your devices. Notifications are optional intrusions.

• Refuse guilt. Laundry can wait, emails can wait, judgment can wait.

• Move slowly, breathe fully, savor a cup of tea, coffee, or cocoa. This is not indulgence—it is strategy.

The first few minutes are often the hardest, because the brain insists on producing a checklist of everything you should be doing. But once you settle, the reward is immediate: clarity, warmth, and the quiet satisfaction of self-respect.

Micro-Rituals of Downtime

Rest doesn't need to be monumental. Micro-rituals are often enough:

- Reading a page, a paragraph, or even a single sentence aloud just because it pleases you.
- Putting on music and letting it fill the room while you close your eyes for a few beats.
- Watching the snow fall—or rain, or whatever the season brings—and allowing your mind to drift.

These are small acts with oversized benefits. They remind you that stillness is not empty—it is restorative, creative, and sometimes even revelatory.

The Rebellious Pause

There is a quiet rebellion in choosing rest. It says: "I will not be dictated to by calendars, to-do lists, or anyone else's expectations. I know what I need, and I will claim it."

This rebellion can be playful: a cozy robe over pajamas at 4 p.m., a long bath with bubbles and no one to report to, or a nap that stretches longer than polite society might recommend. These are not excuses—they are strategic victories for body, mind, and spirit.

Guilt-Free Enjoyment

Rest without guilt also extends to pleasure. That cup of coffee with an extra shot, a favorite pastry, or a favorite TV show isn't indulgence; it's affirmation. It is saying: "I deserve warmth. I deserve joy. I deserve this moment."

For Boomers, this is a skill honed over decades. We know the difference between neglect and nourishment. We've spent enough of our lives doing, fixing, and caretaking to recognize the value of pause.

In Summary

January offers the gift of space. Resting without guilt is not laziness; it is mastery. By intentionally claiming downtime, savoring small rituals, and rebelling quietly against society's relentless pace, we create a month that feels rich, restorative, and entirely ours.

So sip that coffee, curl up with a blanket, let the world move on without you for a while, and smile. Rest is a triumph, and January is the perfect stage for it.

CHAPTER NINE

Resting Without Guilt

January is the perfect month to master the art of resting without guilt. After the holidays, the social obligations, and maybe a playoff game or two, downtime should feel like a crown settling gently on your head. Yet somewhere along the line, society decided that doing nothing is suspicious, lazy, or "unproductive." Boomers know better. We've weathered enough chaos to recognize that rest is not a luxury—it is survival, strategy, and, when necessary, rebellion.

Claiming space for yourself is the first act of courage. Find a favorite chair, a window nook, a cozy blanket on the sofa. The very act of creating a sanctuary, no matter how small, is a quiet triumph. Silence the devices. Let the emails wait. Forget the laundry for a moment. Move slowly, breathe fully, and savor the cup of tea, coffee, or cocoa in your hands. This is not indulgence; it is reclamation.

Rest does not have to be monumental. Micro-rituals offer their own quiet glory. A few deliberate moments with a book, reading a line or paragraph aloud simply because it pleases you, can be restorative. Music filling the room, eyes closed, allowing the mind to drift. Watching the snow fall—or the rain, or the bare branches swaying in a winter breeze—and letting your thoughts wander. These acts are small in effort but immense in reward. They remind us that stillness is not emptiness, but a place where clarity, creativity, and perspective gather.

There is a quiet rebellion in choosing rest. It is a gentle defiance against calendars, to-do lists, and other people's expectations. A cozy robe over pajamas at 4 p.m., a long bath with bubbles and no one to report to, a nap that stretches longer than polite society might deem acceptable—these are not excuses. They are strategic victories for body, mind, and spirit.

Rest without guilt also extends to pleasure. A perfectly brewed cup of coffee, a favorite pastry, a show you've loved for decades—these are affirmations. They declare: I deserve warmth. I deserve joy. I deserve this moment. For Boomers, this is a skill honed over decades. We understand the difference between neglect and nourishment, between the frantic doing of life and the quiet art of being.

January offers the gift of space, if only we allow ourselves to take it. Resting without guilt is mastery in miniature. By claiming downtime intentionally, savoring small rituals, and resisting the relentless pace of the world, we create a month that is rich, restorative, and entirely ours.

Sip the coffee. Curl up with the blanket. Let the world move on without you for a while, and smile. Rest is not a pause in life—it is one of its finest triumphs, and January is the perfect stage for it.

CHAPTER TEN

The House as a Winter Friend

Winter transforms the house. It becomes more than walls, windows, and furniture—it becomes a companion, a silent witness, a co-conspirator in comfort and survival. The air smells of warmth: faint traces of lingering holiday cookies, the soft must of old books, and the clean scent of a home that has been lived in and loved. Outside, the world is gray, damp, or brittle with cold; inside, the house waits, offering refuge, laughter, and quiet counsel.

There is a subtle magic in noticing it: the way the sunlight catches the edge of the armchair, the way the radiator hums like a discreet guardian, the way the kettle's whistle punctuates the silence. Winter exaggerates these small comforts, demanding attention, gratitude, and acknowledgment. It teaches us, gently, that life need not always be a race toward the next obligation or event. Sometimes, it can simply be the rhythm of warmth, reflection, and contentment.

The Optimism Drawer

Every house has one, whether it's literal or metaphorical: a place where hope is kept in small, tidy packages. For some, it's a drawer filled with letters, recipes, or photographs that remind us of victories, kindnesses, and quiet triumphs. For others, it is a corner of the closet or a shelf of books that have carried us through storms. This drawer does not promise grand change; it promises continuity, resilience, and the ability to find light in gray months.

The beauty of the optimism drawer is that it is often discovered unexpectedly. A card from a friend, a note to oneself, a photograph of laughter past—all these items remind us that life, though ordinary, is richly textured. Opening it can be a daily ritual: a tiny act of rebellion against despair, a wink at the universe, a choice to see the thread of hope even when the calendar insists on January's gloom.

And, of course, a little sass is required. If optimism is tucked away, hidden in a drawer somewhere, it does not need to be shouted. It simply needs acknowledgment, like a secret joke between you and the house, or a subtle smirk at life's insistence on throwing cold winds your way.

The Quiet Hope of Ordinary Days

Outside the windows, the world may glisten with frost, or drip with gray rain, or be silent beneath a blanket of snow. Inside, life hums with the ordinary: the hiss of the tea kettle, the soft shuffle of slippers across a floor, the occasional distant laughter or sigh. These moments, small and unremarkable to an outsider, are nothing short of miraculous when you pause long enough to notice.

There is hope in the ordinary, because it is steady and reliable. Bills still arrive, yes, and errands demand attention, but the ordinary days carry the promise of survival, of presence, of grace. There is power in routine, in ritual, in making the bed, brewing the coffee, checking in on friends or pets. These acts are not spectacular, but they are profound. They are proof that life continues, that resilience persists, and that January—gray, cold, and long—does not have to be bleak.

And then, because life is nothing if not deliciously ironic, there is humor. The cat knocking over the mug of tea you just set down. The dog sprawling across the only chair that fits your height. The furnace sputtering just long enough to make you question your choices. These are the small absurdities that keep winter from feeling like a monologue of gloom. They are reminders that wit, perspective, and a little cheekiness are as essential as warmth and blankets.

The house as a winter friend, the optimism drawer, and the quiet hope of ordinary days together form a trinity of survival, comfort, and joy. They are not flashy. They do not demand recognition. But they are steadfast. They are elegant in their persistence. And for Boomers who have navigated decades of seasons, events, triumphs, and losses, they are nothing short of necessary.

So light the lamp, steep the tea, let the house hum, and remember: even in gray months, ordinary days hold extraordinary promise. The house, with all its quirks, warmth, and quiet counsel, stands beside you. It waits, ready for laughter, reflection, and the occasional mischievous act of comfort.

CHAPTER ELEVEN

Why January Smells Like Coffee & Laundry

January smells like survival. Not the sharp tang of panic or the sweetness of holiday treats, but the steady, reassuring aromas of coffee and laundry. It's a scent that says: "We are here. We are awake. We are keeping life together, one sip and one fold at a time."

Coffee, of course, is essential. The first cup in the morning is an act of defiance against the cold, the gray, and the sluggish brain that insists you are too old for early rising. Its steam curls through the kitchen like a warm banner, a subtle herald of optimism and small victories.

Laundry follows—less romantic, but equally heroic. January laundry is the battlefield of winter: sweaters heavy with snowflakes, scarves imbued with the scent of outdoor walks, socks that have seen the long slog through slush. Folding it is a meditation, a ritual, and, if you squint, a quiet form of artistry. Socks paired, towels fluffed, a hint of softness left behind: triumphs in domestic geometry.

The two aromas combine to form the understated perfume of January life: practical, comforting, and slightly rebellious. Coffee says, I am awake. Laundry says, I am competent. Together, they whisper: We will get through this month, one small act at a time.

And while it may sound mundane, it is profoundly human. January is long, the days gray, and the world outside indifferent, but inside, there is warmth, order, and the clever defiance of routine performed well. Add a cat circling your ankles or a dog sprawled across the floor, and the house becomes a living companion in this domestic triumph.

The scent of coffee and laundry is January's signature. It is ordinary, yes, but there is nothing ordinary about sustaining life with elegance, humor, and quiet resilience. In these smells, the month is tamed. The gray outside matters less. The cold is softened. And the small victories —folded laundry, a finished cup of coffee, the day survived—are celebrated with every inhale.

So lift your mug, smooth the sweater, and smile. January may be cold, damp, and long, but it smells like competence, warmth, and rebellion in equal measure. And that, dear reader, is a scent worth savoring.

CHAPTER TWELVE

Pets in Winter (Fur, Whiskers & Snow Boots)

Winter changes the world, but it also changes the way we see the ones we share it with—especially the four-legged companions who make our homes feel alive. Pets in winter are miracles wrapped in fur, feathers, or scales, bearing the cold, the wet, and the snow with unwavering devotion, while quietly teaching us what it means to love without condition.

A dog bounding through the snow reminds us that joy can be simple, urgent, and utterly contagious. Each paw print left in white drifts across the yard like a reminder that small adventures matter, even when the air bites, and the wind stings. Their excitement is contagious, a living antidote to gray skies and January blues.

Cats, meanwhile, are winter philosophers. They curl in impossible contortions on the radiator, nudge your hand when you need comfort, and watch snowflakes drift past the window with the intensity of a Zen master. Their purrs are engines of warmth, small vibrations that say, I am here. You are safe. We are together.

And yet, winter is not always easy. Leashes become cumbersome with snow-packed sidewalks, wet paws track chaos across polished floors, and the cold bites unexpectedly. There are mornings when the thought of stepping outside to clean a litter box or bundle a shivering dog feels monumental. And then you see their eyes— bright, expectant, utterly trusting—and the fatigue melts, replaced by gratitude, patience, and sometimes tears.

For many Boomers, pets are companions in ways that transcend the ordinary. They are silent witnesses to the long nights of January, the small victories of routine, the rituals of coffee and laundry, the celebrations of ordinary days. They know when to offer comfort, when to demand a walk, when to insist on presence. They are fur-covered therapists, comedians, and little sparks of life in a season that can feel endless.

Snow boots, tiny jackets, or simple mittened hands guiding paws through ice-crusted sidewalks become symbols of commitment. It is an act of care, yes, but also a quiet reminder that winter need not be lonely. The world outside may be cold, gray, and indifferent, but the life inside—shared with a loyal companion—is vibrant, warm, and profoundly alive.

Sometimes, when the house is still, and the snow drifts quietly against the windows, you can hear them breathing. And in that rhythm, the world softens. The ordinary becomes extraordinary. The cold loses its bite. A wagging tail, a gentle nuzzle, a soft purr—they are winter's proof that love, presence, and resilience persist.

For those who share their lives with pets, winter is less a season of endurance and more a season of intimacy. It is a time of small joys, shared warmth, and lessons in patience, kindness, and unconditional love. And yes, sometimes it brings tears—soft, grateful, perfectly human tears—because there is no companion quite like one who greets the grayest days with unshakable devotion.

So when the wind rattles the windows, and the frost spreads across the glass, remember to look down. There will be eyes, a nudge, a fur-covered insistence that you are not alone. In winter, that is everything.

CHAPTER THIRTEEN

Friendship Rituals (The Lifelines)

Friendship in winter is more than a social convenience; it is a lifeline. It is the text you send without expectation, the call that interrupts the monotony of gray afternoons, the small ritual that reminds you someone else knows your rhythm, your stories, your quirks. For Boomers, friendships are curated over decades. They are tested in celebrations and crises alike, refined by distance, difference, and time, and strengthened in ways only longevity can create.

These rituals are rarely grandiose. They are simple: a shared cup of coffee, a walk before the streets get slick, a Saturday lunch that stretches into storytelling and laughter. Perhaps it is a phone call that lasts too long, because no one wants to hang up. Perhaps it is a note tucked into a card, sent for no reason other than, I was thinking of you. Each act, small and deliberate, carries the weight of meaning, continuity, and love.

Winter gives these rituals significance. Outside, the world may be gray and cold, the wind biting at your cheeks, the sidewalks slick. Inside, friendship offers warmth, both literal and metaphorical. The comfort of someone who knows your history, who laughs at your same jokes year after year, who offers perspective without judgment—this is the lifeline. It reminds us that while January may feel long, the days are tethered by connection, shared experience, and small acts of kindness that endure.

Friendship also teaches patience and humor. A long-time friend may arrive late, complain about the weather, or repeat a story you've heard ten times before. But by now, you have learned that these quirks are part of the charm. They are the gentle proof that friendship is not perfection, but persistence. It is showing up, in every season, in every weather, in every mood.

And there is mischief, too. Winter gatherings, even intimate ones, are perfect opportunities for small rebellions disguised as tradition. Perhaps you introduce a game, a toast, or a snack your friend swore they would never eat again. Perhaps you invent a ritual just for this year: pancakes for breakfast, mismatched socks for laughter, or a playlist that no one asked for but everyone secretly enjoys. These moments of playful rebellion are woven into the fabric of connection.

Friendship rituals in winter are both practical and sacred. They make the season bearable and beautiful. They remind us that life is not only about surviving gray days but celebrating the warmth that persists in hearts and homes. They teach us that laughter, empathy, and presence are the real treasures of long winters.

So, call that friend. Send the note. Invite someone for a walk, a meal, a coffee that may stretch longer than intended. Celebrate the ordinary, the dependable, the enduring. These lifelines—small, steady, and full of love— are proof that even in January, connection can be luminous, sustaining, and profoundly joyful.

CHAPTER FOURTEEN

When February Sneaks Up

February has a way of arriving quietly, like a friend slipping into the room when you weren't looking, yet it carries an unmistakable energy. One morning, you look at the calendar and blink: the month is half gone, the snow still stacks outside, but the world feels just slightly different. The days are a little longer, the light a little softer, and something in the air whispers mischief and sweetness.

It's the month of red, of cards left on counters, and chocolate that mysteriously appears in desk drawers. A time when even the most stoic among us notice little gestures—a note tucked under a mug, a flower in a vase, a wink in a text. The world seems determined to remind us that warmth, humor, and connection can arrive even in the coldest, grayest weeks.

February also sneaks in with obligations disguised as delight. Dinner invitations, casual meetups, even the subtle pressure of "planning something" can tiptoe in while you're still finding your winter footing. Yet, for Boomers, it is an invitation to playfully bend the rules: show up a little late, bring a snack no one expected, or invent a small tradition that is entirely yours.

And winter sports do their part, too. Playoff fever may still be alive for some, tailgates and snacks offering excuses for indulgence, for laughter, for the shared excitement of being present with friends and family. Chips, wings, and whatever fits in a cooler become symbols of devotion—to team spirit, to camaraderie, and to the simple joy of gathering.

February is not long, but it arrives like a wink: a reminder that life moves fast, that the ordinary can be extraordinary, and that there is delight to be found in both the planned and the surprising. Even in the gray and cold, February teaches us to notice the small sparks—bright, playful, and often a little red—buried amid the routine.

This month, subtle as it is, offers the perfect stage for small acts of humor, generosity, and connection. It reminds us that life is meant to be noticed, celebrated, and occasionally indulged, even if only in chocolate, a toast, or a laugh shared with a friend who knows exactly how silly—and beautiful—these months can be.

CHAPTER FIFTEEN

The Things We Swore We'd Never Do

Ah, the things we swore we'd never do. That list—written in youthful certainty, etched into our mental stone tablets somewhere between high school and our first real paycheck—has a way of laughing at us. Socks with sandals? Check. Drinking decaf and pretending it's satisfying? Guilty. Hosting a virtual gathering because it's "just easier"? Don't look at me like that—I never thought I'd do it either.

January and February are the months that quietly tempt us to bend those "never-ever" rules. Maybe it's the long gray days, the leftover holiday chocolate, or the whispering idea that we are allowed a little mischief disguised as compromise. Whatever the excuse, these small rebellions are deeply satisfying. We discover that bending with style, humor, and wit is a talent we've honed over decades.

And there is joy in seeing the unexpected unfold. That elaborate "never again" recipe from a holiday dinner ends up becoming the perfect mid-January indulgence. That marathon of a TV show you swore you'd never watch becomes a shared ritual with a friend. Rules, it turns out, are often suggestions written in invisible ink—meant to be interpreted creatively, with just enough rebellion to keep life interesting.

Boomers, in particular, excel at this. We navigate the contradictions of life with humor, elegance, and a twinkle in our eyes. We laugh at the promises of our younger selves and embrace the delicious irony of the present. And sometimes, the things we swore we'd never do are the moments we remember most fondly, stories we retell with a grin, and traditions that sneak into our lives disguised as spontaneity.

The lesson? Never underestimate the power of playful compromise. There is freedom in choosing to bend, humor in admitting we were wrong, and delight in seeing the rules we once worshipped transformed into opportunities for creativity and laughter. Life, after all, is far too short to take every "never" literally.

So go ahead: break a little. Laugh a lot. Celebrate the contradictions. Relish in the things you swore you'd never do, because sometimes, those are the best parts of the journey.

CHAPTER SIXTEEN

Walking Through the Door
(Finale)

And here we are, standing at the doorway together — you on one side of the page, me on the other — the same way January itself stands between what was and what will be. If this book has taught us anything, it's that January isn't just a month; it's a hallway. A threshold. A place where we dust ourselves off, roll our eyes at our own dramatics, and walk forward anyway.

But now the door we've been walking through is the last one in this book. And so we pause — because endings deserve a breath. Endings deserve intention. Endings deserve warmth.

This is where I fold my hands to Anjali Mudra, bring them to heart center, bow my head just slightly, and tell you — truly — thank you.

Not the polite, breezy "thanks!" we toss across supermarket parking lots.
No. I mean the kind that comes from that quiet, private place in the chest where sincerity lives.

You showed up for this book.
You walked with me through rituals, mischief, nostalgia, snow boots, coffee steam, soft bravery, and all the January contradictions we pretend to understand.

You gave me your time — which is the most precious currency we have.
You gave me your attention — rarer still.

You gave me the gift of letting my voice into your life for a little while.

And without you?

My craft is nothing.

Zero.

Zilch.

A beautifully wrapped present with no one to open it.

Writers don't exist without readers.

We can scribble into the void all we want, but it's the heart on the other side of the page — your heart — that makes it real.

You are the universe in which this book has meaning.

If any line made you smile...

If any moment made you sigh...

If any chapter made you feel seen, or comforted, or less alone...

Then everything — every word — was worth it.

This final chapter isn't a goodbye.

It's a gentle nudge.

A whispered encouragement.

A wink at the doorway.

Because life will continue to hand you new Januaries.

New rituals.

New contradictions.

New laughter.

New tiny rebellions.

New quiet hopes.

New snowflakes melting on your sleeve before you even notice they arrived.

And when February sneaks up — as it always does — you'll walk through that door, too.

With humor.

With grit.

With tenderness.

With the same strength that carried you through the one before.

So take this with you:

You are allowed to rest.

You are allowed to begin again.

You are allowed to feel everything — and survive everything — with grace and wit and a little sparkle of rebellion.

If January teaches anything, it's this:

Nothing is too late.

Nothing is too small.

Nothing is too silly.

Nothing is too slow.

Nothing is too quiet.

And nothing — nothing — is wasted.

Thank you for reading this book.

Thank you for being its companion.

Thank you for being the reason it exists.

With both hands pressed gently to heart center — Anjali Mudra, my friend.

Walk through the door.

I'll meet you on the other side.

ACKNOWLEDGMENTS

To the quiet hand that polished these pages, unseen but essential.

To the tea, the English biscuits, and the small comforts that made writing possible.

And to you, dear reader, for giving these words a home.

—A. L. Manley

REFERENCES & INSPIRATIONS

Roman Mythology

- Hamilton, Edith. *Mythology*. Little, Brown and Company, 1942.

- Everitt, Anthony. *The Gods of Rome: Religion in the Roman Empire*. Oxford University Press, 2012.

American Holiday & Winter Traditions

- Forbes, Bruce David. *Christmas: A Candid History*. University of California Press, 2007.

- Hester, Jessica Leigh. *American Holiday Traditions: Origins and Evolutions*. Chronicle Books, 2014.

- Bell, Nancy. *The History of Holiday Decor and Lights*. HarperCollins, 2010.

Coffee, Domestic Rituals & Everyday Life

- Pendergrast, Mark. *Uncommon Grounds: The History of Coffee and How It Transformed Our World*. Basic Books, 2010.

- Masuno, Shunmyo. *The Art of Simple Living*. Tuttle Publishing, 2017.

- Clear, James. *Atomic Habits*. Avery, 2018.

Micro-Rituals, Gratitude & Well-Being

- Emmons, Robert A., and McCullough, Michael E. *The Psychology of Gratitude*. Oxford University Press, 2004.

- Csikszentmihalyi, Mihaly. *Flow: The Psychology of Optimal Experience*. Harper & Row, 1990.

Pop Culture References for Boomers

- *The Ed Sullivan Show* (CBS Television, 1948–1971)

- Peanuts, *A Charlie Brown Christmas* (Television Special, 1965)

- *The Beatles Anthology* (Documentary, 1995)

Pet Companionship & Winter Care

- Bradshaw, John. *The Pet Effect: Health, Happiness, and Human-Animal Bonding*. Basic Books, 2012.

- Horowitz, Alexandra. *Inside of a Dog: What Dogs See, Smell, and Know*. Scribner, 2009.

Sports & Tailgate Culture

- Oriard, Michael. *King Football: Sport and Spectacle in the Golden Age of Radio and Newsreels, Movies, and Magazines, the Weekly & the Daily Press*. University of North Carolina Press, 2001.

- Sandomir, Richard. *Sports Memories of the Baby Boomer Generation*. Sports Publishing, 2015.

www.ingramcontent.com/pod-product-compliance
Lightning Source LLC
Chambersburg PA
CBHW022132280326
41933CB00007B/655